A Manager's Guide to the Appraisal Discussion

A Manager's Guide to the Appraisal Discussion

by
Ian MacKay

Cover design by Karen Greville-Smith

Printed by
Crowes of Norwich

British Library Cataloguing in Publication Data

MacKay, Ian
    A manager's guide to the appraisal discussion.
    (Training books for managers)
    I. Title II. Series
    658.3125

ISBN 0851710999

Acknowledgements

We are grateful to Gower Publishing Co. for their permission to
reproduce the Checklists Preparing for an Appraisal, Staff
Development, External Training Courses and Coaching from *35
Checklists for Human Resource Development* by Ian MacKay,
published by Gower in association with the Institute of Training
and Development, 1989.

Cartoons are reproduced by kind permission of Punch.

1. Introduction

Appraisal is a fact of life for many people. Some endure it stoically. Others see it as a temporary, although recurring, nuisance. Yet others see it as akin to a visit to the dentist's surgery involving a potentially painful and unpleasant experience. Indeed, for many people it is an experience which they would prefer to forego, given the chance.

These comments apply equally to the written appraisal and to the subsequent discussion with the manager. This booklet is not concerned primarily with the written documentation however. It focuses instead directly on the appraisal discussion and offers practical help and advice concerning its conduct.

If you have read this far the chances are that you are a manager who conducts periodic review discussions with your staff. If you wish to develop your approach, then this booklet will help.

"Why, Kilburn, how quaint! You want a rise because you deserve one."

2. The appraisal discussion

The discussion is the most critical part of the appraisal process. Whatever other objective it may have in your organisation it must surely aim to consolidate mutual understanding, to stimulate the development of individual members of staff and enhance their job satisfaction. Such development can be achieved by adopting a problem-solving focus without any emphasis on correcting 'faults'.

There are a number of important issues which affect the outcome of the appraisal discussion. These include:

i)   the amount of preparation undertaken independently by both of you before the discussion;

ii)   the degree of participation by the person concerned during the discussion;

iii) your attitude towards the person;

iv)   the effect of any criticism;

v)   the focus of the discussion;

vi)   your overall ability as a manager.

Each is considered in turn.

Amount of preparation

The quality of thought and preparation you undertake before the discussion is critical to success. The same applies to the person concerned. The quality of the outcome is directly related to the efforts of both of you before the event. If either of you approach it 'cold', the discussion is likely to end in failure.

For the person this will include reviewing his or her personal job performance over the appraisal period and the circumstances within which the results were achieved. Such analysis may lead to the realisation that more training or experience is needed in a particular aspect of the work. It may also appear that on reflection there had been more to the job than had been anticipated. This in turn may lead the person to ask the question "Why was I not helped more than I have been?" Both of you should be prepared to address questions of this nature during the discussion.

"No offence, Brother Benvenuto,
but we're putting you back on the bells."

Your own preparation is also critical to success. You can do much to help prepare yourself by considering the questions contained in the checklist entitled 'Preparing for an appraisal' shown on p. 32.

Remember: it is unlikely that a fruitful dialogue will be achieved in much less than an hour. As a result you must set aside ample time for the discussion, which should be conducted in private for obvious reasons. Allow a contingency period of at least half an hour in case the discussion goes on longer than you anticipated. On no account whatever should you allow interruptions during the discussion itself.

Remember also to plan the discussion sufficiently far ahead to allow the person to prepare, and once the time has been agreed it should not be postponed. Finally, don't be late for the appointment - it could be seen as discourtesy or disinterest, or both.

One last point on preparation: choose a time when the circumstances are favourable to both of you. For example, it would be wiser not to schedule the discussion in the middle of a rush job in which you are both involved.

Level of participation

The person's participation in the discussion is obviously vital to success: the greater the participation the greater the likelihood of satisfaction, not only with the outcome of the discussion but also with your own managerial performance. Such participation also tends to promote a more willing acceptance of agreed performance improvement targets and promotes their subsequent achievement.

It is your task to encourage the person to participate, to give him or her the 'air-time' to talk through issues and put forward solutions to any problems. Remember: you are not the focus of the discussion!

You can best encourage the person to participate by asking the right questions and then actively listening to the answers. Both these skills are considered in more detail later in these pages.

Your attitude

You must remember that you will be in the dominant role at the outset and you must therefore ensure that you do everything you can to put the person at ease. Hitting the person with a critical question or comment right at the start will obviously not do so.

"I have mixed feelings about you, Prescott. I'm going to recommend you for a promotion, but I'll see that you never get it!"

It is important to encourage the person to talk freely: you must listen to evaluate not only *what* is being said, but also *how* it is being said and *why* it is being said. Not everyone with whom you hold an appraisal discussion will be committed to it, and it is your job to gauge at what level of commitment the person concerned is operating. If matters you wish to discuss are being deflected, or your words are producing an argumentative response, you must remain calm and patient. Such an attitude of unhurried calm will defuse the provocation and help you to continue the discussion rationally. It is representative of the attitude of an assertive manager, and again is discussed in more detail later.

If you also take on the role of helper, rather than judge, during the discussion, such an attitude will communicate itself very quickly to the person concerned. You can help positively by inviting the person to participate in the discussion and then listening to the responses. When the invitation is accepted, you may only have to summarise what has been said at appropriate moments and subsequently draw the discussion to a conclusion.

One last point on your attitude in this respect: your task is not finished when the discussion is over. You will have agreed follow-up sessions during the discussion and you must ensure that they take place as planned. To approach these sessions positively, not least by actually holding them and being constructive about them, will show just how serious you are about the process of appraisal and will be reflected in the attitude of the person concerned.

The effect of any criticism

Those areas of a person's job performance which you criticise during the discussion are much less likely to result in any improvement. Indeed experience shows that the number of criticisms is positively related to the number of defensive reactions shown by the person during the discussion. This can result in a chain reaction between your criticisms, the person's defensive reactions and lack of commitment to performance improvement.

Adopting a problem-solving focus for the discussion and concentrating on strengths and future developments to which both of you can contribute is much more likely to be productive. One more point: under no circumstances whatever criticise the person's personality - you are not God!

Focus of the discussion

The focus of the discussion should reflect the day-to-day contacts between you to consider progress. These informal contacts provide the basis for the discussion which itself must be forward-looking.

The person's development should be discussed openly and agreement reached subsequently on appropriate development targets in the form of an action plan. (For some thought starters see the checklist 'Developing the action plan' on p 37. Three other checklists which may also be helpful in this context are shown on p 39 et seq.)

Specific time scales should be agreed, but should not normally extend beyond the next appraisal period. Again it must be emphasised that after the appraisal discussion has taken place you should hold frequent informal discussions to review progress with the person concerned.

The actions agreed between you provide the 'yardstick' by which success will be judged. As the manager, your personal contribution to the person's future performance by regular coaching and counselling is far more significant than any off-the-job training course.

Every discussion you conduct should produce mutually agreed action plans for development, the implementation of which must be the responsibility of both of you.

Your overall ability as a manager

The evidence currently available suggests very strongly that a person who is satisfied with your day-to-day performance as a manager is more likely to be satisfied with your performance during the appraisal discussion. This probably will not surprise you, however, because the skills consistent with day-to-day success are those which contribute positively to a successful discussion - open, two-way communication, mutual trust and support, and a helpful attitude on your part.

"He always rewards good work . . ."

An important component of such managerial competence is a demonstrable skill in coaching and counselling people. A manager who coaches his, or her, staff throughout the year will present no surprises at the annual appraisal discussion.

But what about the discussion itself? How would you rate your own skills at handling appraisal discussions currently? Some skills which are particularly important in this context are considered now.

3. Asking the right questions

Many managers are unaware of the range of questions open to them in exploring development issues despite the fact that we all start asking questions virtually as soon as we are born. The standard of questioning at countless appraisal discussions leaves much to be desired.

Reflect on your own use of questions during the discussion in which you are involved. Are you satisfied that you invariably employ the right questions to good effect? Or could your questioning technique be improved? Having thought about it for a moment, are you sure that you know and use the full range of questions open to you? Remember, it is only by asking the right questions that you will achieve the aims of the discussion.

So what are these questions? There are three major types, each of which has a particular purpose, as shown below.

Question Type	Typical purpose(s)
Open	To explore broad background information
	To explore opinions/attitudes
Probe	To show interest/encouragement
	To seek further information
	To explore opinions/attitudes in detail
	To demonstrate understanding
Closed	To establish facts/information

There is also a fourth type of question, called here the counter-productive question, which you should avoid.

Question Type	Typical purpose(s)
Counter-productive	To prompt desired answer To confuse or mislead To prevent the person from saying anything To discourage or indicate bias

Each of these four types of question is described below.

Open questions

The object of asking open questions during the discussion is to encourage the person to talk freely. For this reason they are sometimes referred to as non-restrictive or indirect questions. The person concerned is in no way restricted in his or her choice of answer and is unobtrusively given the opportunity to say as much as he or she likes. Open questions are particularly useful during the initial stages of a discussion to promote a good atmosphere and to 'set the scene'. They are also an effective way of introducing new topics during later stages of the discussion.

The general open question is perhaps one of the most useful questions available to you, primarily because it helps to introduce or 'open up' a particular topic. It is sometimes called the 'Tell me about' question as this is the phrasing habitually used by many managers: for example - 'Tell me about what happened when...?' and 'Tell me, how did you deal with that situation...?'

Probe questions

This type of question, as the name implies, is designed to search for information in much greater depth. Sometimes called 'follow-up' or 'focusing' questions, their main object is to get beyond the (possibly) more general replies to open questions and to consider development issues in more detail.

Of course this does not mean that probing should be carried out like an interrogation. If you assume the role of insensitive interrogator, such an attitude will certainly offend and embarrass the person, or at worst provoke a positively hostile reaction. Obviously you will not try to 'break' the person, although you may need to explore some of the aspects of job performance which he or she might prefer not to discuss.

Throughout the discussion the atmosphere should be one of calm, friendly enquiry. The establishment of such an atmosphere through judicious use of open questions will pave the way for a more detailed discussion without the probe questions seeming to be intrusive. As in many other social situations what you say may be less important than how you say it.

Closed questions

The purpose of using closed questions is to supply you with specific items of information. The person is severely restricted in his or her reply and has little chance to develop a theme. As a result it requires very little effort from the person and correspondingly more from you.

Nevertheless, this form of question tends to be overused in discussions not least because such questions are easy to phrase and are apparently time-saving. In the past, much advice has been given to novice managers about not using closed questions. However, such questions can be helpful to you principally in verifying information, and also in directing the discussion back towards its mutually agreed purpose.

Counter-productive questions

Any question which plainly detracts from the purpose of the discussion may be called a counter-productive question. If you remember that it is your job to help staff members to talk in order for the purpose of the discussion to be achieved, then any question that suggests the 'right' answer, confuses or misleads, or prevents a response, will have the opposite effect. Such questions should be avoided at all times.

"Tell me, Smithers, if all the world's a stage, how come all the clowns are employed in this office?"

The straightforward lead is one example amongst many. This question form is usually phrased in terms of a clear emotional appeal, which is why it is sometimes called an 'obvious' question. The straightforward lead begins with phrases like:

'You have got to admit that...?'
'Isn't it a fact that...?'
'You must concede that...?'
'You will acknowledge that...?'
'You cannot deny that...?'

'You wouldn't say that...?'
'You don't think that...?'
'You are not suggesting that...?'

Each is designed to produce a definite 'right' answer. In every case the questioner's appeal is 'Please tell me what I want to hear - I am making it as easy for you as I can'.

Now consider the fuller list of questions open to you which is shown in Fig 1. Do you use a wide spread of these types of questions? Or are your questions predictable? Your answers will indicate just how much you may need to develop your skill at asking questions during an appraisal discussion.

When you are asking questions, do not forget the following points:

● Keep the purpose of the appraisal discussion clearly in mind.

● Use plain language.

● Allow thinking time for response.

● Maintain an atmosphere of friendly neutrality.

● Do not talk too much.

The quality of your questions will be reflected in the quality of the responses they generate. Some types of questions are particularly useful in helping you to judge the emotional tenor of the discussion. Accurately gauging the degree of commitment is critical to success and is considered next.

Fig 1   Types of questions open to you

QUESTION TYPE	PURPOSE	QUESTION FORM	ILLUSTRATION
OPEN	To explore broad background information	General	'Please tell me about...?'
	To explore opinions/ attitudes	Opinion-seeking	'What do you think about...?'
		Trailer	Making a broad comment on a subject and then pausing in anticipation of a response.
PROBE	To show interest/ encouragement	Non-verbal noises	'Hmm?' 'Ah?' 'Oh' Allied to head nods, etc.
		Supportive statements	'I see...?' 'and then...?'
		Key word repetition	Repetition of one or two key words to encourage further response.
	To seek further information	The pause	
		Simple interrogative	'Why?' 'Why not?'
		Extension	'How do you mean?'
	To explore in detail opinions/attitudes	Opinion-investigating	'To what extent do you feel that...?
		The reflection	'It seems to you that...?' 'You feel that...?'
CLOSED	To establish specific facts/information	Yes/No response	'Are you...?' 'Have you...?'
		Identification of person, time, number, etc	'How long did that job take?' 'When did that happen...?'

4. Testing reactions: gauging the degree of commitment

You have been counselled to choose your questions carefully, and as you are aware there are a number of types of question open to you. These questions are rather like the keys on a piano: played in the right order they can produce a pleasant melody. The reverse is also true: if played in the wrong order (or even in a heavy-handed way) they will produce an unpleasant disharmony for the person who is on the receiving end.

Even if you play the right keys in the right order you may still be unsuccessful if the piano is out of tune. This can happen if you incorrectly assume a basic willingness to answer your questions. Consider the 'ladder' shown in Fig 2: you may expect the person to start at point X on the ladder because this is where you would like to start. If in reality he or she is firmly located at point Y further down the ladder such conflict, if uncorrected, would be a recipe for failure.

This is why open and closed questions are so useful to you during the appraisal discussion. The responses will allow you to gauge the degree of commitment, to establish why the person feels apathetic, anxious, is avoiding an issue you want to discuss, or is even being plainly argumentative.

A word of caution: because you may have gauged the degree of commitment accurately during the opening stages of the discussion does not mean that it will necessarily remain static throughout. As different topics are aired, the person's commitment may change and move up, or down, one or more rungs of the ladder. Your task is to interpret such moves sensitively and act accordingly, much like an accomplished pianist feeling the way through an unfamiliar piece of music.

Fig 2   Gauging commitment to the discussion

ASPIRATION	...I want to go on and do better	
ACCOMPLISHMENT	...now having achieved success	
ASSESSMENT	...then let's check whether we did it the right way and how we can do better next time	
ACTION	...and decide what should be done and then do it	X
AGREEMENT	...so let's talk about it	
ACCEPTANCE	...and I accept that I will be involved in the solution	
ACKNOWLEDGEMENT	...but now I'm convinced...	
ARGUMENT	...and that is what I will argue, even if I get angry	
AVOIDANCE	I recognise a problem exists, but it's not mine,...it's theirs,...or it's those others...or someone else	Y
ANXIETY	...I do know and I feel nervous	
ANGUISH	...I don't know what it's about and I am worried	
APATHY	...I don't know what it's about and care less	

It is also worth remembering that even if it takes what you think is too long to help the individual move off the lowest rungs of the ladder, it is still time well spent. Without acknowledgement by the person concerned of the issues, and an expressed willingness to talk about them, the discussion will undoubtedly fail.

Such expertise in interpreting and evaluating the (perhaps) shifting degree of commitment, and adjusting your approach as appropriate, is dependent on two other skills which you will find extremely useful in conducting the discussion: being assertive and listening actively. Each is now considered in turn.

5. Keeping your cool: being assertive

Fig 2 illustrated the 'ladder' of commitment, the lowest five rungs of which identify some rather negative reactions which a person might display during the discussion: apathy, anguish, anxiety, avoidance and argument.

Dealing effectively with any, or all, of these reactions is perhaps one of your most demanding tasks as a manager. It is easy to make progress when mutual trust is present and you both adopt a realistic, problem-solving approach to the discussion. It is not so easy if the person does not want to know, feels over-anxious, is 'ducking' the issues, or even arguing the toss with you.

"Frankly, Mr Forsyth, I could do this job standing on your head."

Sooner or later you will have to cope effectively with such a person who may perhaps even unconsciously needle you into getting angry or even losing your temper. Alternatively, depending on your personality, the provocation may tempt you to cut the discussion short on the grounds that the person is impossible to deal with. If you do surrender to such emotions then the discussion will have failed - and so will you!

So how do you prevent yourself from surrendering - from being submissive? The answer lies in staying cool and calm even when you are under pressure, and it is called being assertive.

One of the marks of the truly assertive manager is the ability to absorb criticism calmly without giving offence or reacting with an emotional counter-attack. Such an ability cannot be developed overnight: you need to accept that you are not perfect, do not always make the right decision, and do not know everything. However, if you can acknowledge such imperfections, both to yourself and others, then you have a firm base for action.

So how can the assertive manager - you - accommodate any criticism by the person with whom the discussion is taking place? Some possible responses which you might use are shown in Fig 3. The responses are all examples of what might be called 'reactive assertiveness'.

Fig 3 Absorbing criticism: reactive assertiveness

Criticism of what you do	Criticism of what you are	Criticism of what you know
Accepting criticism by acknowledging that there may be some truth in what is being said, whilst still retaining your right to remain your own judge of what to do.	Accepting your 'faults' by agreeing openly with any criticism of what you are, but without having to apologise.	Accepting your 'ignorance' by agreeing with its presence but, again, without having to apologise.
'Yes, perhaps you're right.' 'Yes, it does look as if I made a mistake there.' 'No, perhaps I shouldn't have done that.' 'Yes, I can see from your point of view that...'	'That's true, I can upset some people.' 'Yes, I accept that I can be insensitive sometimes.' 'Yes, I do tend to burn on a rather short fuse when that happens.'	'No, I don't know the answer to that one.' 'Yes, perhaps I ought to have found out about it before now.' 'Yes, it is a new area for me.' 'Perhaps you're right that I should know.'

Another way in which you can be assertive in the discussion, not reactively but proactively this time, is by aiming for mutually acceptable solutions to bridge any gap between your views and the views of the person concerned. This aspect of being assertive hinges on the use of the word 'we' and shows that you are committed to a joint approach:

'Could we crack the problem this way?'
'How about doing this first and then following up with...?'
'What if we approached them to get their ideas initially and then we could...?'
'Would it be better if we...?'

These are all examples of hypothetical questions, the 'What if...?' question - which can be particularly useful not only for exploring alternative tactics in this context, but also for showing that you are prepared to make part of the running without imposing your views.

You are giving the person every chance to participate in the discussion, to think through the issues and make an equal contribution, and avoiding phrases like 'You must...', 'I think you should...', and 'I want you to...', which show that you are imposing your own views. Remember, no one will commit themselves to a decision fully if they do not 'own' it, and such ownership depends directly on involvement.

Helping a person to become more involved in the discussion may test the skills of asserting yourself in another way. If the person is being apathetic then you can practise another form of proactive assertiveness: patiently and calmly repeating your words until the person recognises your insistence and that you are not going to let the topic drop. The following extract from a hypothetical discussion illustrates how this form of proactive assertiveness may be used:

> "Now,...I'd like us to discuss the reorganisation issue."
> "...but that's nothing to do with me."
> "Yes, I understand that you believe it has nothing to do with you, although I'd like us to discuss it."
> "...now hang on, I've been up to my ears in the C35 project and it's taking all my time."
> "I know you've been fully occupied on the project. I'd like us to talk about the reorganisation issue."
> "...but the others have more time...and it's more in their line anyway."
> "You may be right...now about the reorganisation."
> "Look dammit...it's your problem, not mine."
> "I accept that it looks like that from your point of view but nevertheless I'd like us to talk it through."

By calmly acknowledging the other person's point of view this head of department is refusing to be diverted from the wish to discuss the reorganisation. The red herrings are accommodated within each response, but without any form of provocation or aggression which themselves would provide the opening being sought to divert the discussion elsewhere.

Proactive assertiveness of this kind is a powerful weapon in the armoury of the assertive manager although it must be used wisely: only when the situation really calls for its use and when there is no other alternative. In any event it requires considerable skill at listening to, and interpreting, what people are saying to be truly effective. This skill is considered next.

6. Listening to the answers

Are you a good listener? Are you significantly better at listening than the average person? If you are not, then you will not contribute effectively to the discussion. Why? Because the average person does not listen well at all. There is a great deal of evidence to suggest that straight after 'listening' to a ten minute oral presentation the listener has only understood, evaluated and retained about half of what was said - and it is not long before half of that has been forgotten! If your listening ability is no better, then you are denying yourself the chance of real success as a manager in this context. You cannot be a good manager if you do not listen.

Most people confuse the ability to listen with the ability to hear. They take it for granted they can listen. This is not the case. Remember the old saying - hearing is with the ears, listening is with the mind. You need to listen with your mind (and for that matter, with your body, as we shall see shortly). Merely to hear what is said is not enough. So how can you improve your listening ability and achieve better results?

Perhaps the most effective way is to pay particular attention to what psychologists call your 'attending behaviour'. Indeed this phrase sums up a number of the skills you need during the appraisal discussion. There are two types of attending: the physical and the psychological.

Physical attending

Physical attending - listening with your body - means showing an attitude of involvement - showing the person that you are 'with' him, or her, just by your physical attitude or posture. You can show your involvement in a number of ways:

● Facing the person squarely.
● Keeping good eye contact.
● Maintaining an open posture.
● Leaning forward slightly.
● Remaining relatively relaxed.

Each of these points is helpful in showing the person that you really are listening. Each one sends out small vibrations and shows that the message is receiving your undivided attention.

"Really? . . . Wholesale ironmongery . . . how fascinating."

For instance, facing the person has this effect. It shows that you are concentrating on what is being said. You are 'seen' to be listening because you are directly facing the person concerned. Good eye contact will also reinforce the 'I am attending' message. Of course it does not mean using a wide-eyed unblinking stare. Anyone would find such a look totally disconcerting. What it does mean in practical terms is looking at the person's eyes rather more than perhaps you generally do now. Apart from anything else it helps to minimise the intrusion of visual distractions.

However, facing the person and maintaining eye contact are not enough on their own. To really show you are listening, you should also adopt an open posture and lean forward slightly. A good illustration of these points is shown by your stance when you are listening to 'good' news, whatever it might be. You are 'all ears', you do not want to miss a word! You are not sitting with your arms folded, glancing at your watch, inspecting your fingernails, or doing anything else which will put the speaker off. You are quite still, leaning forward slightly so that you miss nothing. You are not just 'lending an ear' - you are offering both unconditionally. This is what happens when you really want to listen, and this readiness communicates itself very clearly, especially during a discussion of this sort.

There is one final point associated with physical attending - being relatively relaxed. This does not mean being so much at ease that you look as if you are about to drop off! And obviously it does not mean appearing rigid, tense or drawn in on yourself as some novice managers have a tendency to appear to be. To be relatively relaxed involves showing a calm but interested exterior, and this physical composure will quickly communicate itself to the person concerned.

These points in total are what physical attending is about. But it is one thing to be aware of what you should do, it is another to put it into practice. Do persevere. Improving your physical attending will have a marked effect on your listening ability and will help you to improve your performance as a manager in this context. But physically attending is only one side of the coin. The other is psychological attending, which is considered next.

Psychological attending

Paying attention to the factors involved in psychological attending will help you to build on the physical attending skills described earlier. In mastering these attending skills you will be developing abilities which are of crucial importance to you.

So what is the key to these psychological skills? In a word - concentration. Psychological attending is all about concentrating - not only on what the person is saying but also on how it is being said, and what is not being said.

To concentrate on what is being said means listening for the central theme, rather than the 'facts' which are notoriously difficult to remember anyway. It means using the difference between the speed at which you can think (about 500 words per minute) and the speed at which the person is replying to your questions (probably around 120 - 130 words a minute).

You therefore have 'spare capacity' to think ahead of what is actually being said. If you use this spare capacity wisely you will have time not only to mentally review and evaluate the response but also to assess how complete it is. You also have time to frame your next question carefully, to probe deeper if you are not fully satisfied that you both understand each other. But this is only possible if you really do make the best use of your superior speed of thought.

To think ahead in the way described above means keeping an open mind, staying neutral. Indeed it might be a good idea if all managers had the words 'stay neutral' indelibly inscribed on their minds! If you can keep such an open mind and remain neutral you will avoid being side-tracked from the main purpose of the discussion, namely to agree ways in which the person can gain greater satisfaction from the job by extending his or her job performance.

You will also find it easier to interpret the person's tone of voice and other non-verbal messages which may provide clues to any gaps in what is being said.

A diagram illustrating a range of non-verbal signals is shown in Fig 4. Having studied the diagram, take a moment to consider how your own non-verbal signals might be

interpreted. Is your self-presentation everything it might be
during the discussions in which you are involved?

Fig 4

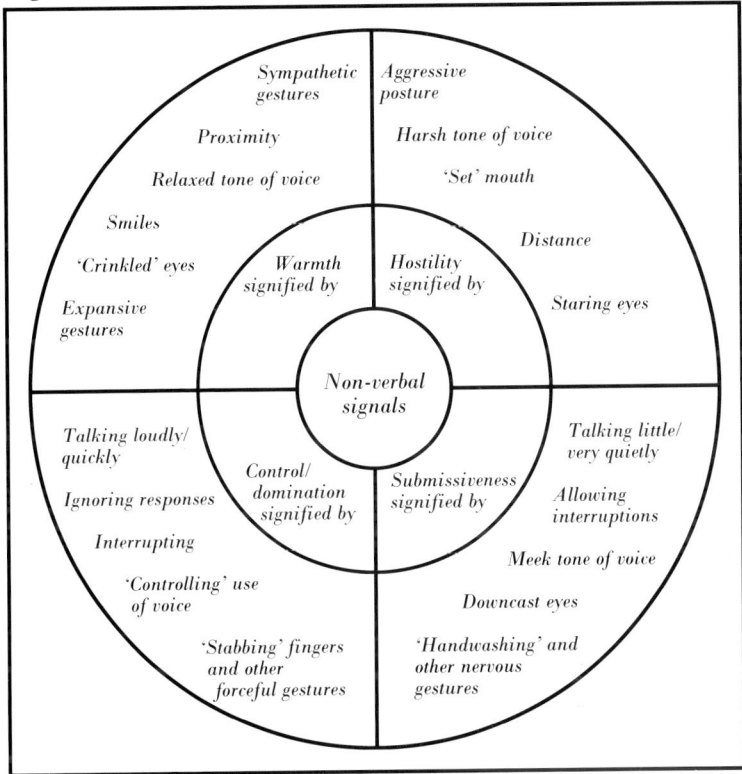

Many people are unaware of the effect their non-verbal
behaviour may have on others. Indeed, the following
approximate figures give some indication of the relative
importance attached to the component parts of a speaker's
message:

Words	10%
Tone	35%
Non-verbal behaviour	55%

Suffice it to say that if your words are in conflict with your non-verbal behaviour, it is the latter which will invariably be assessed as genuine by the person concerned. And a final point - it is well worth taking a few brief notes of what is said during the discussion. Listening can be a particularly strenuous activity as has been noted previously - your concentration can lapse.

"Can't I plead with you, Helen? It isn't my wish that our marriage should end like this."

So, to summarise these crucial skills, help yourself to listen by:

Physically attending which involves

LOOKING INTERESTED Facing the speaker.
Maintaining eye contact.
Keeping an open posture.
Leaning slightly towards the speaker.
Staying relatively relaxed.

and

Psychologically attending

BEING INTERESTED **Listening to what is being said by:**
Keeping an open mind.
Thinking ahead.
Analysing and evaluating the message.
Getting the full story.
Not interrupting.
Not talking for more than about a quarter of the time.

Listening to how it is being said by:
Interpreting the person's tone of voice.
Evaluating the non-verbal signals.

Listening to what is not being said by:
Listening 'between the lines'.
Searching for possible gaps in your understanding.
Asking the right questions.

7. Epilogue

The foregoing pages provide some flavour of the skills you need if you are to conduct truly effective appraisal discussions. And if the discussions are approached and conducted in a spirit of mutual trust and understanding then their aims will be better achieved: the people concerned will want to improve their personal contribution to success and will gain a greater satisfaction from their jobs and the process of appraisal. When this happens you will be discharging your managerial responsibility for helping people to grow in both their own and the organisation's interests.

"Mr Johnson, I feel I'm entitled to a little more of the gravy."

8. Further reading

E. Fear **The Evaluation Interview**
(McGraw Hill, 1958)

I. MacKay **A Guide to Asking Questions**
(BACIE, 1980)

I. MacKay **A Guide to Listening**
(BACIE, 1984)

N. Maier **The Appraisal Interview**
(Wiley, 1958)

Checklist:
Preparing for an appraisal
Background considerations

1. What are the stated aims or purposes of appraisal in your organisation?

2. To what extent do you 'massage' the formal aims towards what you think they ought to be? If your answer is 'not at all', are you sure?

3. Do you accept that periodic review of the performance of your staff with them is an integral part of your job as a manager?

4. Are you fully committed to the process of appraisal? If not, what are you saying about your own chances of promotion in the organisation? And about treating your staff fairly in this respect?

5. Are you fully competent to discharge your commitment?
   - How many days training have you undergone in relation to appraisal processes?
   - How long ago did the most recent training take place?
   - When was the last time you read an article or a book on the subject?
   - What action, if any, do your answers suggest?

6. Are you absolutely sure you appreciate why the appraisal is to be conducted?

Preparing for the appraisal itself

7. What information do you have by which you will judge
    the individual's performance?
    - Is it really sufficient from your point of view?
    - Is it enough from the individual's point of view?
    - Assuming a self-review is an integral part of the
      procedure, have you studied the individual's response
      in detail?
    - If a self-review is not carried out, why not? Is the
      individual sufficiently involved? Is review something
      done genuinely with people, or merely about them?
    - Could you request a written self-review in this case?
    - Are you now truly in a position to make an objective
      assessment? Are you sure?

8. What actions were agreed with the individual for this
    appraisal period? What priorities were agreed?

9. Which parts of the job were particularly testing? In
    what ways?
    - Time needed?
    - Time available?
    - Personal application?
    - Ability?
    - Interpersonal skills?
    - Or what?
    Why? Was it planned? What is the individual's view?

10. Just how far was the individual's performance affected
    by circumstances? Did these circumstances help or
    hinder performance? How? To what extent?

11. What is your overall view of the individual's
    performance?
    - How well has the individual performed against each
      target?
    - How closely does your view compare with that of the
      individual?
    - Was more achieved than you expected? Or less? Why?

- Which tasks were performed particularly effectively? Less effectively? Why?

12. What particular abilities has the individual utilised in performing the tasks? How could these abilities be developed further?
    - What action could the individual take personally?
    - What joint action/commitment could be agreed?
    - What personal commitment from you may be appropriate?

13. What particular lack of ability may have prevented the individual from achieving success? As a result, what specific action could be taken to ensure success in the future?
    - By the individual?
    - By you?
    - By both of you jointly?

14. What, if anything, is the individual doing in relation to his or her own self-development?
    - On whose initiative?
    - What does your answer indicate about the individual's approach to the job?
    - What part should your answer play, if any, in the written appraisal? In the subsequent discussion?

15. What scope is there to develop the job? To what extent has the individual done so? How far does it seem the individual might do so in the future?
    - What action, if any, do your answers indicate? On the individual's part? On your part?

16. How often have job-related progress discussions taken place during this appraisal period? With what effect? Have the discussions been reflected in extended performance? What reference should be made to this aspect in the written appraisal?

17. Having considered the background to this particular appraisal in broad terms, are you now in a position to

complete your detailed analysis of the individual's performance during the appraisal period? Do you recognise that the quality of your analysis will affect directly the quality of the subsequent discussion with the individual?

18. What possible tasks and priorities for the next appraisal period should be covered during the discussion?

19. How should the discussion be structured? What do you want to include? What may the individual want to discuss? What should the agenda be? Are you absolutely clear in your own mind what has to be covered? And in what order?

20. At what point will you inform the individual of the place, date and time of the appraisal discussion?
   - Will you ensure that the individual has sufficient time to prepare?
   - Is the timing favourable? For both of you? Are you sure?
   - How will you ensure that the discussion is conducted in private and that there will be absolutely no interruptions?

21. Are you sure you will have allowed sufficient time in your diary for the discussion?
   - Have you allowed a contingency period within the time (say half-an-hour) to ensure that the discussion is not interrupted?

22. If you have allowed less than $1\frac{1}{2}$ hours in total for the discussion, are you sure you are giving both of you the best chance to succeed?

After the discussion

23. Was your planning effective? Did the dicussion achieve its purpose? How do you know?
   - Are you satisfied?

- Is the individual satisfied?
- Was mutual understanding and commitment achieved?
- Did the discussion have a positive outcome?
- Have the follow-up sessions been positive?
- If there has been no follow-up, are your responses to the first two questions in this checklist still valid?

24. What have you learned during your preparation, and the subsequent discussion, which will be of benefit to you in the future? What specific steps will you take to ensure that any learning will not be dissipated over time? What else will you do to extend your performance in this respect? When? How will you monitor your own progress?

Checklist:
Developing the action plan: considering the possibilities

The agreement of realistic, achievable action plans for individual members of staff is critical to the success of any appraisal programme. One way of considering the possibilities, before the discussion, is to review the following five-step approach to staff performance and development.

STEP 1   Have you agreed/defined the overall purpose or objective of your section/department? Have you established what the individual's job is in relation to the section/department's objective? Is this purpose accurately reflected in the person's job description and in the appraisal documents?

STEP 2   What should be the individual's major priorities for the next review period? What factors, outside the individual's control, could prevent success? What action/support is appropriate on your part?

STEP 3   Within each major priority what should be the key tasks be? (Successful completion of these tasks will result in achievement of the priority.)

STEP 4   What performance standards are appropriate for each of the key tasks? What should be agreed jointly in terms of:

Quantity - How much?   Time - By what time?
Quality - How well?   Cost - At what cost?

Remember: use of ambiguous words like those shown below will not be helpful in completing the action plan.

'Adequate'	'Reasonable'
'Approximately'	'Minimum'
'Few'	'Desirable'
'As soon as possible'	'Satisfactory'

These words define nothing.

STEP 5   What specific help/guidance could you give to support the individual in achieving particular elements of the action plan? How will you make absolutely sure that both of you understand precisely what these points are?

Checklist:
Staff development

1. Do you accept that it is one of your prime management tasks to help your staff develop their job performance?

2. To what extent could the job performance of many, if not all, of your people be improved? How specific can you be? Have you considered in detail their individual strengths? Areas of competence? Areas of possible development? Are these questions considered with them? Or merely about them?

3. Do you personally devote sufficient time *now* to considering the on-going development needs of your staff?

4. When was the last time you carried out an audit of development needs in your department? Would it be worth doing again now?

5. How do you identify the individual development needs of your people? Do you start by considering the major areas of possible development?

Focus of action	*Targets*
Remedial	Improving particular aspects of performance which are not up to standard for whatever reason
Developmental	(a) Reinforcing personal strengths (b) Acquiring new skills and knowledge to cope with future work challenges
Innovative	(a) Developing better ways of dealing with existing tasks (b) Discovering ways of dealing with new tasks

6. Is the situation discussed, and agreement reached, with the person concerned on appropriate development targets?
   - Are the results to be achieved stated clearly?
   - Are specific time frames agreed?

7. How often do these discussions take place with individual staff? Is that often enough?

8. When considering the possible methods of reaching the targets, do you recognise that on-the-job development invariably makes a much more significant contribution to success than off-the-job training courses?
   - What is the balance, both qualitatively and quantitatively, between off-the-job training and on-the-job development activities in your department?
   - Are you satisfied with the answer?

9. Which of the following development activities play a significant role in your department? Which ones could be used more? Or introduced for the first time? What is the overall balance? Is it acceptable?

Special assignments/working parties/projects
   - Would special assignments to investigate specific problems for defined periods of time add to the individual's knowledge and experience?
   - How should such assignments be monitored?

Committee assignment
   - Would such assignments broaden experience and knowledge, and increase confidence in achieving results by negotiation and discussion? How could such assignments be arranged? Could the individual deputise for you?
   - How should progress be monitored?

Coaching and guidance
   - Which individuals might benefit particularly from your personal help?
   - What help, specifically, is appropriate?

- What pre-planning is necessary?
- How might fruitful discussions be set up? And 'learning contracts' agreed?
- Do you possess the inter-personal skills appropriate to be an effective coach?
- What is your relationship now with the individual(s) concerned? Does a firm base for coaching exist already?
- How should progress be monitored?

Job rotation/secondment
- Would the individual benefit from broadening/ updating his or her technical knowledge/experience? Supervisory/management experience?
- How critical is the need?
- Would rotation within the department meet the need? If so, when? For how long?
- If not, could secondment to another department/ division be arranged? To a supplier/customer? To some outside agency? Again, when? And for how long?
- In any event, how should progress be monitored?

Study for formal qualifications
- Should the individual be encouraged to study for further technical or professional qualifications?
- What are the possibilities of encouraging the individual to join an organisation-based distance learning group (eg Open University, Henley Distance Learning programme)?
- How close are your ties with local higher education establishments? Are you aware of the opportunities on offer?
- What monitoring is appropriate?

Membership of professional societies
- Should the individual be encouraged to participate actively in a particular professional society? To stand for office to gain wider administrative/ managerial/public relations experience?
- How? When?

Planned delegation
- Which of your present responsibilities/tasks might provide a valuable learning experience for individual members of staff?
- How should these tasks be delegated? Verbally? Or in writing?
- To what sort of approach would each individual react best?
- Will all those concerned be made aware of the responsibilities you have delegated?
- Will you leave the individual concerned to get on with the job? Will you also delegate the right to be wrong?
- Will an attitude of 'watchful neglect' be appropriate on your part?
- When the tasks are completed, how will you evaluate the effect of your delegation?
- On the individual? With the individual?
- On yourself?

Mentoring
- Has the possibility been considered of appointing 'mentors' (i.e. helpers) from amongst your more senior staff to assist in the development of inexperienced staff?
- Which of your more experienced staff might also be helped to develop themselves (development-by-self) by assuming the role of mentor to particular individuals (who would experience development-of-self)?
- If such a possibility has not been considered, should it be? When? Who else should be involved?
- What monitoring would be appropriate?
- If 'mentoring' is an unfamiliar term, what should you do? What will you do?

Planned self-development
- Are individuals actively involved in their own self-development?
- If not, would it be worthwhile asking everyone to conduct a written personal assessment of their own

contribution to departmental efforts? And to prepare
subsequently a proposed action plan for discussion
with you before implementation is agreed?
- What monitoring of self-development plans takes
place currently? Should such monitoring be
extended?
- What more could you do to extend the impact of
self-development as a staff development tool? What
should you do? What will you do?

Off-the-job training courses
If a training course appears to be the most (only?)
effective way of meeting a particular development
need, how will the most appropriate course be
chosen?
- On reputation?
- On cost?
- On availability?
- Or what?
- Will the individual concerned be fully briefed before
the event?
- Will agreement be concluded on
  - why attendance is considered appropriate?
  - what your expectations are concerning pre-course
  preparation? On return from the course?

10. What other possible development methods not
mentioned above could you use to encourage a more
critical self-awareness of personal performance standards
amongst your staff?
- How can you encourage them to be more proactive
about their learning? How can you help them to
develop their approach to on-the-job learning?

11. What action do you intend to take now? What targets
do you intend to set yourself? What steps will you
take to extend your commitment to helping your people
develop themselves?

12. How willing are you to commit yourself to discussing progress every week with at least one member of your staff?

13. How much time will you devote each week to reviewing overall progress and formulating appropriate action plans? Half an hour? An hour? More?

14. How will you monitor your own self-imposed development targets?

Checklist:
Using external training courses

1. Have the training needs of the individual(s) concerned been identified? Precisely? For instance, if a supposed communications training need has been identified, what particular type of communication is involved? Verbal? Or written? If written, is the need to improve performance in writing memos, reports, business letters or what?

2. How was the need identified? Was it done by consultation? With the individual(s) concerned? By whom? If it was not immediate supervision, why?

3. Is the need for:
   - Initial training?
   - Booster training?
   - Retraining?

4. Having pinpointed the training need, have you also identified the standard of performance required as a result of the training? With those concerned? Have the criteria of success been established? Have these criteria been quantified when possible?

5. Once the parameters have been established, have you examined thoroughly all alternative methods of meeting the need? On a cost-effectiveness basis?

6. If, as a result, using an external training course appears to be the most effective means, have you considered the following points?
   - How many staff need training?
   - For how long?
   - When should they be trained?

- What are the priorities?
- How should they be trained?
- Where should they be trained?
- At what cost?

7. Have you considered, on a cost-effectiveness basis, the possibility of mounting an in-company course with the help of outside speakers to fill the training need?

8. What would be the other advantages of this approach (e.g. a tailor-made course concentrating on your organisation's policies/practices/needs)?

9. If this approach is not appropriate, how do you choose the most suitable external course?

10. Does your organisation maintain a 'register' of courses on offer at different levels and for different occupational groups?

11. Who is (or should be) responsible for its regular updating?

12. Are you aware of the various bodies which provide information on course availability (e.g. your industry's training board, regional management centre, the various professional institutes, research associations, etc)? Is your organisation on their mailing lists? If not, what action should be taken? By whom?

13. How is the effectiveness of particular external courses checked? If assessment does not take place prior to use, why not?

14. When a particular course has been chosen, is the individual concerned briefed fully before attending the course? Is agreement reached with him or her on:
    - Why attendance is necessary?
    - What is expected in terms of pre-course preparation?
    - What is expected during the course? And on return from the course?

15. When the individual returns from an external course is

he or she asked to prepare a critical report on the course against the criteria of success established at the outset? If not, why not? If so, who is responsible for reviewing the feedback and following up with any necessary action? Is it done? By the right person?

16. During the last financial year, how many employee days were devoted to external training? How does this figure compare with that for training carried out within the organisation? What were the total costs of each type of training? How does each figure, and the total, compare with the organisation's sales turnover in the same period? Was it too much? Or too little? Against what criteria?

17. Is your organisation really getting its money's worth from using external courses?

Checklist:
Coaching - an integral part of management

1. If you are a successful manager, what have been the significant factors in your success? Was one factor the positive help (guidance, coaching, counselling) you received from senior managers?
   - Are you still getting, or would you benefit from, further help now?
   - What does this answer indicate?

2. How seriously do managers in your organisation take their responsibilities for developing staff?
   - Are they really aware of the implications of this responsibility?
   - How do you know?

3. Are they devoting as much time as they should to developing the performance of their staff? Are you?
   - To what extent is 'coaching' regarded as an integral part of every management job?
   - Do all managers help to develop the performance of their staff by:
     - Systematically giving them planned tasks to increase their abilities and experience?
     - Evaluating their performance in relation to these planned tasks?
     - Giving appropriate *personal* guidance to sustain/develop progress towards the target?
     - Generally monitoring performance against the time-scale set?
   - If not, what action is indicated?

4. Has a check ever been made in the organisation to establish just how much training individual managers

have received in coaching techniques?
- How many individuals have attended practical
  training sessions outside the organisation on the
  subject? Have any been conducted inside the
  organisation?
- How many work days were involved last year?
  How many so far this year? Spread over how
  many managers?
- Is that really enough when the critical importance of
  every individual's contribution to success is
  considered?

5. If the (further) commitment of managers to the
   advantages of coaching is to be gained, has the practical
   application of the technique in your organisation been
   fully explored?
   - If so, by whom? With what results?
   - If not, who should be responsible for doing so?

6. Have the following question areas been explored?

Strategy
7. What are the main areas within individual
   departments which could provide opportunities for
   coaching?

   The work itself
   - What are the major problems currently? Potentially?
   - Which can be used to provide a practical learning
     situation for staff?
   - Have the opportunites for coaching been positively
     identified?
   - Can targets (end states) be derived from these
     opportunites and closely specified?

   Individual staff
   - What shortcomings in attitudes, skills and/or
     knowledge have been identified, and need to be
     overcome?
   - Can targets for improvement/development be
     specified?

8. Can coaching priorities be set, based on the above?

Tactics
9. Considering the priorities in order, what action is appropriate to meet individual learning needs in terms of:
    - The situation itself?
      - What pre-planning is necessary?
      - Have the main constraints been considered?
      - Will the relevance and value of the assignment be made absolutely clear? How?
    - The personality/skills of the manager concerned?
      - Interpersonal skills?
      - Listening skills?
    - The personality of the individual concerned?
      - Existing skills and knowledge?
      - General capability?

10. What timing and specific coaching approach do these answers suggest?
    - What will be delegated? How? When?
    - Will the appropriate authority to act be given?

Control
11. How will progress towards the targets be measured? What yardsticks are appropriate? What feedback is necessary?
    - Will the control be flexible and amenable to modification?
    - How will each individual's thinking be stimulated? Can the control be by watchful neglect?
    - Could such an approach help to build a sense of trust?
    - Will each individual be given every chance to monitor his or her own progress?

Further action
12. If managers are committed to this approach, would it be worthwhile evaluating their use of coaching by periodically asking them the following questions? And

asking these questions of yourself?
- What positive plans have you for coaching each one of your staff in the next six months?
- What lessons have you learned from recent coaching situations? Are you applying them now?
  • Has your own management style developed?
- What benefits has coaching produced in your department?
  • How does individual performance now compare with what it was six months ago? Twelve months ago?
- If it has not improved markedly, are you really spending enough of your time on coaching?
- Do you truly believe that by helping your own staff to grow you are growing yourself? If not, what does this answer indicate about your own managerial prospects (see question 1)?